Comity

Comity
Nations and Nature

PATRICK RYAN

COMITY
NATIONS AND NATURE

iUniverse books may be ordered through booksellers or by contacting:

iUniverse
1663 Liberty Drive
Bloomington, IN 47403
www.iuniverse.com
1-800-Authors (1-800-288-4677)

ISBN: 978-1-5320-0004-1 (sc)
ISBN: 978-1-5320-0005-8 (e)

Library of Congress Control Number: 2016910438

Print information available on the last page.

iUniverse rev. date: 06/23/2016

Contents

Pre-ramble

There are about two hundred bones in your body.
There are about two hundred countries on earth.
So can we all make one big plea
And make this thing work from birth?

Your body is about 70 percent water.
The earth is about 70 percent water.
We need to make the right kind of stir
To make life genuine and pure.

The brain has two hemispheres.
The earth has its own north and south.
We just can't always play it by ear.
We need more than word of mouth.

The comity of nations depends on respect.
It takes mutual consideration and courtesy.
We can't live in our own little sect;
Ruling for the many is the key.

The law of nature is about thinking, feeling, and acting.
The nature of ruling is more for self-interest.
Where one is more about gracefully aging,
The other is more about being able and biggest.

Just as the human body is invaded by disease,
The earth has only known war and peace.
But we have always been able to find cures,
So it follows that we can live secure.

What is important in all affairs,
Whether a personal or state objective,
Is to do right and to know justice,
As it can be profitable for our heirs.

Laws are not made for proud reasons,
And force of arms does not always bring cohesion.
Where major decisions need to be made,
We must watch for the danger of
errors and let reason pervade.

We all have a bundle of natural rights,
And all men are prompted by their nature.
As animals, we look for an advantage.
As thinking beings, we must stay engaged.

It engages us to procure the good of others,
Not in any manner whatever, but with morality,
Because for all men to feel most free,
We must regulate according to community.

Even other animals have their cares,
Be they political, sacred, or of despair.
In the final measure, when all is compared,
We need a faculty of principles to prevail.

In some form or manner, a sense of
belonging extends to us all.
There is a sentiment of value to a person enthralled
With a clear and evident impetus
For self; both internal and external.

It is a sense of heart that brings just and right
And fear of wrong that we need laws to fight.
By linking heart and fear, we can conceive
Of content for all and a good future life.

At times, the spear and the sword are necessary.
But remember—virtue itself can be justice.
Fortitude is needed for wisdom and pleas.
Care and integrity can spring forth thus.

Rules of engagement are for nations,
Rules of virtue and fortitude for nature.
Rules rule nations by decree
But know their nature like you and me.

Personalities bring color to any set of rules,
And for those true to commonality of purpose,
They have an advantage over the fool.
Their commitment to rules makes them firm.

Endeavors to promote knowledge of law
Are an example of method and fewer flaws.
Authority of law can only be upheld
If those with knowledge gently weld.

Speak not of things hard to understand,
But be a force for the rule of good.
If we can do this, then objective truth withstands
Over different times and scopes and for all manhood.

For this kind of discourse to pervade,
The nature of vice must be mislaid.
Liberty has a tendency toward ideas,
And the liberal man gives for many eras.

Multitudes of people live and exist.
All want the same basic things from life.
The problem is we are not comingled but subsist.
It is from these subcommunities that nations rise.

In these many nations exists the body of people,
Whether a private person, elected official, or king.
Some are more influential in setting a code that is civil.
Some speak of truths that ring.

It is important how the body relates to the nation
And how nations relate to other bodies' conditions.
A body or nation has the right of war
In order to treat a condition or sore.

War is seen as an end for its purpose.
The end result must, of course, be peace.
War, acts of hostility bring combat to us
And last until opposition happens to cease.

We, the body and the nation, do not want war with injustice,
But we need to do what we think we must.
These are concerns for each side and combatant
So can both be justified while disenchanted.

Is it nature to take from another to enrich oneself?
Probably not in itself, but each depends
on welfare as a whole,
And while one body or nation may think of just the self,
Another may believe defense of equality controls.

The right of war is that done without injustice,
As all members of the human body must attest.
Some govern, and some are governed accordingly.
Some have superiority, but all the right of equality.

Who profits from such a thing?
When called to arms by a faculty,
Some answer to the power; some to the act.
And natural rights must be one's own, in fact.

The rights taken between two or more
Must evince a capacity and aptitude,
Because when we delve into acts of war,
All our faculties should be grounded in rule.

Strictly taken, war is for the fit and decent
And not a fiction, contract, or affront.
Attributive concepts are proportioned among,
So our acts are not forbidden and out of zone.

Actions must oblige the body and nation,
And our nature's served as a matter of virtue,
Because when we raise arms and take action,
Our meanings, motives, and morals must not be skewed.

The law of nature is normally unalterable.
Some are of the mind to be right and reasonable;
Some are just intrinsically evil.
Each must be judged according to the law of the sovereign.

Murder and theft, for example, are crimes,
But in times of war, they become benign.
By nature, we are all at liberty,
And that gives one the right of force to stay free.

We all, by nature, try to observe the law,
Unless by evil we have a flaw.
This is true of the body and those who rule;
When rulers injure, the body must not be fooled.

Proof of necessity is not always certain,
And some rules hide behind a magic curtain.
In a democracy, we expect full disclosure.
In a one-rule regime, knowledge is a slur.

We all begin with the human and civil.
When we treat others, we should watch not to cull.
When we recognize wrong for what it is,
Our vigilance must be maintained with some bliss.

Disputes, by nature, are fraught with errors.
Side against side start out as blamers.
If discourse or actions show no relief,
We are obliged to rule, and our nature we must keep.

The law, evolved, is a written thing.
The law, through religions, lies in the heart.
Therefore, the law is our conscious and our being,
And our thoughts have meaning, but only in part.

For the parts of the body politic
Taken as its whole measure,
Between thought and action, there will be conflict,
And rights and privileges can be peculiar.

Silence alone can be prohibitive.
If, as they say, good men will allow
That which is otherwise forbidden,
We all must work to find the right know-how.

Bare facts must remove the hindrances
That are contrary to the body's conscience.
The temporal sovereigns of a people
Should encourage the artful and able.

For what the law of a nation allows—
Be it defined by boundaries or beliefs—
The law of nature must be reavowed,
And only then can the body feel relief.

Virtues are required by all different churches,
Such as patience, charity, and especially humanity.
So with good reason and research,
We can all be pious, just not blindly.

Man is fitted for both peace and war.
He was given hands, but not a spear.
The nature of the body does not condemn war,
But what is repugnant to the body—beware.

There is a difference between attack and defense.
When terrorists attack, times are tense.
As the body can accept that lawfully done,
Society, remember, is not up for auction.

Those who bring fear in the name of God,
In this day and age—some think them a fraud,
For motives of self-interest still can exist,
But for the most part, we say no to the cultist.

We have come a long way in body and nation,
And nature is more aligned, thanks to communication.
The blood of the innocent is no longer tolerated
As we have evolved, chartered, and crafted.

War still exists, both public and private
Conflicts among natures and nations.
Danger will always threaten, as does a bullet,
And death before one's time still causes a stun.

As always, those who act by their own will
Can change a family or a state balance and axle.
And notwithstanding all else,
We must find a proper place for ourselves.

Governments

There are five main friends in the neighborhood.
Some get along just fine, and some are up to no good.
There is a sixth soul who comes and goes.
When he's around, the five must be on their toes.

Royalty has been around the hood for quite a while.
Democracy moved in later, with a shake and a smile.
Communism and socialism have had their ups and downs,
But when totalitarianism moved in, all five had frowns.

Anarchism is the sixth man in town.
He moves around with the real estate flow.
Some families don't like to see him around,
But sometimes he has been known
to help the body resound.

Royalty lives well and has a big family.
They own many properties and rule by decree.
They can seem nice when they use their discretion,
And they like formalities, for protection.

Democracy puts on a face, less austere,
But around the neighborhood, it is quite clear
That they belong to a family that is functional
But too fussy; freehanded, they like their nickels.

Communism and his cousins try to be close-knit,
But sometimes his authority does not fit.
Sure, in theory, he sounds really good,
But party rule can be intrusive on the body, in all likelihood.

The socialist family had all its property owned by one.
The driver seemed to be handicapped in steering the funds.
Improvements to specific homes could not be made
Without all the houses in the hood in on the same trade.

When the totalitarianisms moved to town,
They made much noise and quite a big sound.
They were the poor kids on the block,
And they didn't much care to be mocked.

Royalty and democracy seemed to get along well,
As each liked to see the means of production swell.
The monarch was glad to, from time to time, sit back
As long as the economy stayed on track.

A dollar spent was its own vote
To buy a goat or a brand-new boat.
As a rule, the free hands were an industrious bunch.
They never wanted to experience a crunch.

In the communist section of town, they liked a mix.
They could hang around with the free-hand chicks.
The totalitarians were economically upside down,
But thought their images were still well renowned.

Well, before long, as one may figure,
Finances seemed to act as their own ruler.
As it got harder and harder to keep up with the Joneses,
The communists altered to the free-hand side, while the
totalitarians paid their mortgages with family hides.

The village had evolved into cliques beyond school.
Instead of all staying on the same page
and with the same tools,
The reasons for this could be well understood.
Some were selected, others elected; some used
force, and others inherited their rule.

It is the nature of the body to strive for preservation.
Rulers of nations are part of the body whole.
The body will lie, cheat, steal, and kill to stay alive,
For such is the primal nature, regardless of our roles.

What deters these primal natures is the paying of dues.
Being out of step with the body can cause a bruise.
We have evolved our nature to let the mind rule.
Unless we can get away with otherwise,
the law we will choose.

When rules choose a nature that the body can't,
It is in the name of the state, so we give grant.
Those who rule and still act in interest alone
Do so by throne, birthstone, or the body's groan.

Many nations have evolved their rule with a mix that works.
To lift the body up, pragmatism has its perks.
A little bit social, communal, monarchal, and democratic
Has been necessary for nations and
natures to meet their basics.

Some states or rules of same
Don't want to change, so others they blame.
They like their rule and the powers that be.
They provide the only vision for the body to see.

They stay dogmatic to keep the status quo.
They use the police, army, and
bureaucracy to keep all in toe.
Censorship of knowledge helps keep the dogma alive,
But he who Rules Magic Bridge between
the world and body never thrives.

In the village of Pittshire, the royalty
chose to live on the north side.
They had a long history and were steeped in tradition.
The hamlet of Hamlin was run through with pride.
There was always much to be done, and
there was not much friction.

Those of the democratic state of mind
Chose the west side of Pittshire and called it Wellington.
Folks seemed nice, for if one stepped
out of line; there were fines.
The bodies worked hard to get ahead
and to feel like they'd won.

Those who chose to live in the communist mix
Lived on the east side of town in an
area known as Secundum.
Their way of life was well known and classic—
Not the wealthiest group in town, but
thought they were second to none.

The -isms authoritative and totalitarian
had the south side, Circum.
The body there stayed pretty much to itself.
Only their chieftains could stay in touch
with the village Fulcrum;
It was a dark part of town with limited
utilities and bare shelves.

Some sons of the village thought they saw a better way
And wanted their say, so they jumped into the fray.
They wanted what others worked their
whole lives for and wanted it today,
So in the name of God, they became
anarchists and looked for new prey.

One thing that was acceptable to all
Was innocent profiting with no harm to the body,
So any advantage from use of a brawl
Usually brought refuting—this time, by three.

The anarchists sought legitimacy from necessity.
They said their backs were to the wall.
Many had fled the dark -isms just to be free.
Immigration aside, they were showing some gall.

As marauding youths in gangs and packs,
The anarchists claimed to be victims as they sacked,
But they went too far when they did invade,
As if they were on a legitimate crusade.

It is here to be noted that many things
are tolerated by nature,
But the laws of nations can bring censure
To those who attach without provocation,
Other than prior devastation from a dark throne.

Nations can and do respect nature.
They even opened up their enclaves to receive.
It was the acts of violence on their lands
That brought their wrath and made them mad.

Even though the anarchists had no state,
They created an apparatus with all the usual traits
Of command, control, intelligence, and an army.
With propaganda and recruitment, they made their plea.

They wanted only what should be common to all mankind,
But they went about it with arms and force,
And their cause became misaligned,
As even those who help an underdog could not endorse.

Some say they felt the burden of loss
When the sovereigns brought forth their own chaos.
But really, the anarchists had little to lose;
They only gave back what was taken, and they still pursued.

With no treaties in place, they could hardly demand
To widen their bounds by space and land.
So if territory was out, they still wanted minds,
For they thought and believed they had plenty of time.

Pluralism

But right now, I really must digress,
For there is something important to all of us.
Just as the body must work in unison,
Nations are better when practiced in pluralism.

Pluralism is the most important word to know
Both from within and without a body
nation, both friends and foes.
We have lived in a pluralistic society since World War II,
And in the twenty-first century, this has never been truer.

From the small parts of Pittshire
To the four corners of the world,
Only the truly astute will aspire
To live and evolve as one, unfurled.

Everything in our world relates;
Math, science, transportation, communications all donate
To that which makes us whole, one, and enabled
To function more ably, in step, and great.

Conflict is a multiorganic and mechanical thing,
And influences of competing interests are not always in sync,
But through significant factions all contributing,
The body, nature, and nations may realize equilibrium.

When we ask the larger question of who governs,
Let's hope we don't all think alike,
Because as time passes and the world turns,
We need diversity for balance and for our psyche.

Just as a river may form a boundary between entities,
Pluralism allows for diversity and
supports increased bounties.
It helps all to gain access to materials and wealth
And reduces a central system for the body's health.

Great difficulty will always arise with such a prescription,
And privatization will be shifted to and from nations.
Multiculturalism, interdependence, and
globalization cannot be denied,
So it is better to allow in stride than to chide.

History shows us that we can take two paths:
We can take a stance not to bend and show our wrath,
Or we can absorb to increase our might.
And future generations want a life that's bright.

Better to bend than to break,
And the benefits we recognize will give all a stake.
To validate our coexistence is hard enough,
So central power cannot forever rebuff.

As it takes a village to raise a child,
So it takes social estates to be closely dialed.
Foundations and principles must always remain,
But the service of rule must take multiple cues.

It has taken a lifetime for our body to reach this point,
And only a few nations are still out of joint.
Clearly, the need to get on board is there,
But the means to do so causes all a scare.

It is one thing to all agree on the rules,
But no body or nation likes to be schooled.
The time for 100 percent participation is still not here,
But let's stay prepared for the day when we are all squared.

Competition must always remain.
It propels progress so we don't stay the same.
Conflict and competition can work hand in hand
And promote a life that our heirs will understand.

If the lifeblood of inheritance is based on a will,
Then the will of the body can make the state fulfill
The concept of a place for all who toil
And follow the golden rule.

Pluralism evolves over space of time.
It should help bodies and nations climb,
For our human society has created great devices,
And our alterations should help our advices.

Just as the body is related to the politic,
It is a part of everyone to use their logic,
Yet for a long time, the intention of nations
Has not always supported the nature of man.

As the toe bone is connected to the foot bone
And the neck bone is connected to the head bone,
The bones are connected to the muscles and blood,
The heart and head, all working to make us rounded.

And so it is with pluralism that there must be
A supply and a chain that links nations and seas.
Bodies and nations need good coordination
And need to provide each with legitimation.

Interorganizational relationships must work
Hand in hand with information for our perks.
Transportation is connected to communications,
As trade between the body and nations
helps for a smooth run.

Computers and the Internet have become an aid,
And we can all expand ourselves with free trade.
Equilibrium and balance are always key,
While tariffs and barriers are sometimes in need.

It is the nature of both body and nations
To want the height of good quality and fortune,
Yet this must be achieved through civility and law,
As to do otherwise brings only delays and war.

A tidy home must first be in place
Before looking elsewhere to increase our base.
A sewer system and electrical grid must not limit
Our roads and armies from performance due to budget.

We, as a world of bodies and nations,
Must keep strong our essentials and rations
Because expansion does not always mean more room,
And our trade should serve to help us bloom.

Multiculturalism

A part of pluralism is multiculturalism,
For if one really believes we are all joined at the hip,
Then, in general, we are all in a partnership,
As we all want our own certain freedoms.

We want to be free to marry, travel, and vote;
Freedom to procreate gives all of us hope.
This has been done, over time, step by step,
And failure to allow these rights is a big misstep.

To be multicultural, both our nature
and nations must accept
Traditions associated with groups that vary.
Acceptance and promotion are good precepts,
And they are a two-way street to grow vicariously.

Ideologies and customs are differently practiced
And can be integrated, assimilated, and righted.
Segregation is not a long-term solution;
It leads to hard laws, differences, and even guns.

While no nature or nation is perfect,
A purist approach restricts growth, trade, and wealth.
Better to have a colorful and valid mosaic
Than to kick and trick and try to remove.

We are already a multicultural global society.
It is only the bounds of pain in establishing
An extended capability and benefit for all to see
That introduce new and vibrant familiarities.

Easy entry and exit into the marketplace
Helps every society and the human race.
Global diversity is now within grasp.
The Internet and Cloud have brought
us to a border-free place.

There will always be critical and well-grounded remarks,
But we all benefit from knowledge that drives commerce.
We can never overlook professions that provide the bulwark
Of raising new generations that will be well immersed.

As we grow globally, we'll have more diversity—
Over time, hopefully, much less adversity,
For commonalities will accrue to one and all,
And civility, not arms, will be the norm of the law.

Interdependence

Interdependence is two or more persons or things
Dependent on each other, with or without strings,
For the body, morality, and physicality come to mind.
Nations, as a reflection of the body's
nature, are also similarly integrated.

Interdependence should not be considered as peculiar.
It is not arbitrary but determined by a mixture.
Just as the vendor needs the vendee,
The global community must recycle
wealth for its well-being.

Commonality can often regulate actions.
Science and the heavens work as one.
Motion and force in nature are based on defined laws,
While morality and political power are
based on interest, sometimes flawed.

When we trade oil for arms, the money boomerangs.
Each tries to join and divide while getting ahead.
For nations to fall behind, the leaders can cause some pain,
So nations become parts of others to continue their stead.

There are all sorts of organizations
with dependent members,
As no body or nation alone can be the only barterer.
Each entity steps back sometimes to
separate immersion and individuality,
As the nature and effect of an alliance are
obligations that sometimes climb high.

Overall, interdependence ventures for liberty,
But engagements we undertake can
also keep us from being free.
Our freedoms, therefore, are based on a balance with thee,
While our strides and forward gains
can sometimes be blistery.

The conditions of the body and nation
are based on limitations of nature,
For self-preservation must naturally inhibit some behavior.
Fear of incurring a penalty or harm
Can force us to re-create our charm
to succeed without arms.

Although it is not our nature to submit to punishment,
If we are joined in organizations, we must try to cement
The entity that safeguards our own sovereignty
While keeping the nation's body's individuality.

Globalism

Globalism is pluralism at its finest.
When the bodies and nations work in concurrence,
Trust is key, and we move forward in unison,
All acknowledging each other in the broadest.

Alienation is lessened, and business traffic is crafted.
It is a process that is integrated among people.
Private enterprise plays a big role,
And nations share their resources with control.

Investment and information have more flow,
And momentum of trade helps all play by the rules.
It's a process that will evolve over generations to come,
And no nation's nature will want to
be left out, as a rule of thumb.

Natural reason dictates a balance for one's own comfort.
Technological advancements make the world smaller.
Nations discover more of one another and wonder less
As we move with more ease between
barriers and increase access.

But nations, like bodies, will always be a little covetous,
For it is our nature to think of our own aloneness.
We all realize a free-market economy is best,
But there still exist rulers who don't care about the rest.

From the days of wooden ships, trade has been king.
Public affairs are not always easy in everyday living.
Each body and nation has its own inclinations,
Due mainly to a long history of a specific orientation.

One would think that equity in trade should apply,
But we are still a world of demand and supply.
Regulation is coming around through organization,
But sometimes, force can bend will
when self-interest must be done.

More and more, technology spins the axis of power,
For it is not always might that proves who is right.
Force of character gives way to long-term goals.
Protection and advancement of the body help nations grow.

Continuity and succession are important aspects.
Accumulation of information helps all connect.
We all are aware that nations are not equal;
Steps can be made to help equalize and make able.

The foundation for globalization is cohesion.
Although it cannot be achieved in our lifetimes,
We can increase and develop our collective education
Where human rights, culture, health, and
environment can more fully shine.

Corporate vs.
Philistine Lifestyles

The largest influence of a nation is its body.
A nation gets its support and stability from thee.
It can also undergo change and upheaval if not pleased,
Or a ruler can repress some but not all, if it is crafty.

For those who rule autocratically,
Their top-to-bottom apparatus must divvy.
The police and army are given a corporate journey
While the have-nots must struggle along gloomily.

A corporate lifestyle takes care of one's needs.
Food, clothing, and shelter are basic for all families.
Physical, emotional, and financial safety helps with esteem.
A feeling of belonging engages one's loyalty.

Philistines today are not the same as in the days of yore.
They tend to be conformist in seeking
comfort, and much more.
Their political engagement is reality
TV and sales at the store.
Can they really be counted on in times of war?

Philistines seem to dwell more in nations with abundance.
Their taxes help the whole to keep a balance.
Hunting, fishing, and high tech are their pastimes.
They care for politics only if they interfere with primetime.

Obviously then, Philistines are not always a majority,
Especially in nations whose rule seems pejorative,
So the body politic in nations so poor
Is still more engaged than in the top four.

Nations that do have a body with Philistines let leaders rule
And have not states still trying to control the schools.
Either corporate or Philistine, each is a tool.
Neither really has the pull to overrule.

There are certain truths in everyone's life—
Some more favorable and significant with less strife—
But there are old sayings common to us all:
"What goes around comes around" and
"Mother Nature can alter the draw."

So if it's a new car or just food on the table one wants,
The body looks to the nation to fulfill nature's needs.
Some nations do have the capacity to succeed
If the body stands vigilant, engaged, and on guard.

Migration and the Economy

The world and the body are always on the move,
Usually brought about by conditions we don't approve.
Sometimes, something new is started for rule.
Most often, the displaced will join another's pool.

In the days of yesteryear, newcomers were welcomed.
In modern times, folks aren't always so gracious.
They feel the job market and economy will be bottomed,
But as it turns out, the extra workforce is a plus.

In recent decades, the new have been absorbed.
If many of the same culture arrive,
productivity hikes are observed.
Specialization can occur in certain geographical areas,
Oftentimes doing work newly created in the work arena.

Migrations in great numbers usually happen with a pattern.
Most want something better and are very concerned;
They are able to discern just what it takes
To get along, provide for family, and not make mistakes.

Economic outcomes associated with these flows
Do not, in the long run, impact employment woes,
Because, in the end, everyone and everything grows,
And total gains outdo losses as we superimpose.

Productive efficiency is enhanced when one wants to work.
Capital intensity helps technological levels perk.
Whether it's in the field or on an assembly line,
The growth helps strengthen the body's spine.

Because we love our property, as is our nature,
We also like the use of our nation's infrastructure.
As we grow, we are grounded to a foundation
That expands our loyalties to the family and nation.

I think you'll find, without looking too hard,
That multiculturalism is more profitable than pure.
Whatever comes into the world is part of us all,
And innovations usually rise after a fall.

According to the law of nature, once mixed together,
They do not separate but transfer into a larger supplier.
To immigrants, we grant not only personal predilections
But depend on the newcomers for national inspiration.

Evangelism and Religion

Religious indoctrination has always struggled
For the hearts and minds of the body.
It has conducted warfare in the name of angels
And now, as times have changed, must do so more smartly.

Christians and Muslims have a steep history,
Buddhists not quite so prominent in scope or bodies.
Public spreading of the Gospel by preaching
Has had its success in gathering through teaching.

Although some nations will not admit it,
Religion and politics fit like a mitt.
The body's morale needs hope for life and beyond,
So most nations have chosen a religion with which to bond.

Converting others can sometimes be an ordeal
And usually works best with use of great zeal.
But there are bounds that conduct should not exceed
Because form over substance can mask the true creed.

Today, some Muslim or Islamic factions
Are going overboard in their actions.
They try to recruit like the Bloods and Crips
And make converts compete to show their spirit.

As all religions have their own hierarchy,
Islamic cells call themselves a state without geography.
Others feel the effects of their divine vengeance,
And they disrupt the body's balance with their license.

This type of Islamic guidance shocks the conscious
As the spreading of the Word with use of ordinance.
They put their rights before those of the sovereignty
And have alienated many and caused many to fear and flee.

They have gone so far as to turn evangelism on its ear,
And many Muslims are converting to
Christianity for a life clearer.
So many deaths over so many years
Have caused great numbers to seek
personal liberty in a new sphere.

So the bottom line is, regardless of place or rank,
Once judged, truth and justice, we cannot forsake.
As the world turns and as time goes by,
Even religious leaders are accountable to apply
The same tenants that all religions qualify
To give hope, keep holy, and help purify.

War of Ideas

War is the state of contention between entities.
Coke and Pepsi have been at it for years and without armies;
In fact, much of war in our times and going forward
Will be fought not with arms but with our words.

War is all around us every day of the year,
From what beverage we drink to what clothes we wear.
We, as nationalists, trying to keep our bodies okay,
Are even contentious over where a product is made.

A war of ideology can involve more than just attitudes.
Its operations can cause damage to a body's turpitude.
Everybody belonging to a nation certain
Needs its own commonalities as its power certain.

When the head of the body is under attack,
The body needs a dose of commonality to keep on track.
What the nation does should be a reflection,
A replication, of the body's liberties—a manifestation.

The nature of war, within communities and beyond,
Brings about change in relationships for bodies and nations.
For reasons social, economic, or political, each state responds
With a propriety and decorum of distinct and ready legions.

War implies some sort of underlying confusion.
When communications of ideals are not in unison,
War is a clash of values that are central and core,
Reflecting an ambition or duty that gives a body rapport.

The cause of war is based on one's determination,
One's purpose, reasons, and culture by one's own operation.
When threatened or intimidated by adverse implications,
A groundswell will rise to resist, to struggle in opposition.

The body needs the head by nature for its peace.
When one's humanity is imposed upon, we naturally police
Viewpoints and ethics that assault our mortality,
So a just war is a variance of commonly held necessities.

War is a collective and coordinated thing by nature.
Usually a type, class, or kind of character
must be of a certain temper.
The commonality of the body and nations gives credibility
To one while assailing another's underlying authority.

The most important part of war is the
winning of hearts and minds,
As it is only then that a succeeding
peace can be well defined,
So a good communication plan must be foremost
To give expression to one's bona fides to the utmost.

Internet and satellite are valuable tools
To inundate and indoctrinate one's symbols and codes
To justify one's protocols, rules, and laws,
Some will say influencing one's cause
while exposing the other's flaws.

To support an opinion, one must give testimony to reason
And be obligated to keep promises of intents and cautions.
What is generated by communication
has a psychological effect,
And the actors are wise to honor and respect.

The law of nature is that one who promises justly
And does not provide evenhandedly or correctly
Will bear the blame and shame of discredit,
And the opposing view will gain momentum and credit.

We all must examine our stance on what we want,
For that will determine our compass and response.
We must choose a side and leave another view behind,
Because in the end, we must know
our own heart and mind.

Peace (Coexistence)

Coexistence means that even when our interests
Or ideologies differ, we can still be in harmony
And maintain our own loyalties as nationalists,
Which is not against our nature or psyche.

The mind of the body and nation can distinguish,
And alteration of design need not prove blockish,
As there need not be fault in change or difference,
As conformity can give rise to concurrence.

In order to enter into various notions,
Nations have the power to alienate or not.
Relief can be reached as a lasting solution
Founded upon a presumption that peace be thought.

Advantages will always be tried for gain,
Both publicly for image and privately in vain.
Publicly, a full display of the nation's goods is accepted;
Privately, a veil on virtue may be a necessity and adept.

Pluralism depends on peaceful coexistence.
Navigation and trade are part of a common precept.
We are naturally partners in some particulars
While legitimately enjoined to foreign fervors.

Ours is a mixed and compound set of axioms.
Actions taken must respect our future condition.
Respect for future time means we take pains to guard
The things we share—our acts and our wards.

There are many reasons to act in concert.
Effects against hazards and casualties are averted,
And the more our nations come in contact,
The more all contracts will naturally
demand a more equal part.

All promises bring limitations to all nations and bodies.
When we discharge what we swore to do, we stay healthy,
And mutuality of respect for sovereignty stays hardy,
For territorial and internal bodies have guarantees.

At their simplest, coexistence and agreements ensure
Less infringement and lessened difficulties
before a mishap occurs.
Being aware that business proceeds as you expect and think
Means damage and confusion will shrink.

Treaties gain and conclude with order.
Natural rights are observed within borders.
Express understandings help overcome weak memories,
And common ground gives rise to increased courtesies.

Reciprocity vs. Comity

Comity and reciprocity can go hand in hand,
Both in theory and their applicability;
However, with some allowances for degree,
One is a courtesy while the other more compulsory.

Comity is a courtesy of international law.
It is a formula that gives equity some convention.
It compels what common interests we long foresaw.
When there is respect among
sovereignties, it lessens tension.

When one nation and body gives faith and credit
To anther nation's internal law, customs, and practices,
Its nature expresses a coherence that is embedded
And makes treaties and alliances less fractious.

To bring order to all when crossing state lines
Helps bring a constant sense of safety and well-being
And helps the world's commerce and money lines,
Although, as a courtesy, there is no absolute guaranteeing.

Whether put to state affairs or as a tourist in a strange land,
A sense of reassurance can bridge what one should understand.
International trade and business can sometimes much pressure,
So to have less stress about rules can make our outlook fresher.

No law has any effect beyond its borders,
So comity allows for a more effective world order.
The world evolves but will never stand still or fixed,
And as we learn what we want, what is good, we intermix.

Personal liberty is number one in a body's life.
Without liberty, our existence is not measurable or right,
So to approve and ratify agreements for one's own land
Helps broaden our life, and our liberties expand.

But for any agreement to be good and valid,
Comity brings logical legitimacy to nature as well rounded,
And as comity depends on the goodwill of all,
Its performance brings peace and prevents pall.

For comity to work, acts must not be done in vain.
Value and worthiness produce goodwill and mutual gain.
Obviously, two can interpret a single event with differences,
But order and comity to guide, we can use common sense.

Reciprocity can be equally complex and significant.
It says what another does for us, we should do in kind.
Reciprocity is both physical and
psychological in dominance,
And its treatment between body and
nation depends on normal inclines.

When reciprocating, one should not go
too far one way or the other,
Or do nothing at all, because to not give back or cover
Has negative effects, expectations always loom,
And we are all expected to repay for balance and by rule.

To build continuing relationships and conventions,
We must do nothing contrary to upset the mechanism.
Reciprocity is the concept by which nations justify
Use of carrots or sticks on the stubborn or Bligh.

Reciprocity, as its basest, is an eye for an eye.
Comity is to act out of goodwill in attempts to glorify.
Reciprocity can be retaliation or seeking reprisal.
Comity seeks to amend and provide
balance for such requitals.

As we become more interdependent and global,
Efficiency is better served by a network more noble.
Reciprocity and comity, like sticks and carrots,
Affect our cognitive behavior and impel merit.

Reciprocity provides balance and equilibrium.
It can cause and affect rejoinder in whatever may come.
It can be a deterrent, restricting and limiting,
As the cost of reciprocity can affect
income, country, and king.

For what is equally deserved is the essence of equity.
Although it does not make all or any equal,
It does provide the body with a natural symmetry
And provides that the intentions of
competition be made more adeptly.

While comity tried to establish an atmosphere of harmony,
Reciprocity can often punish and make yielding.
By our natures, we know what is prohibited,
So thoughts of national advancement
should be exposed when exhibited.

When one tries to enrich at another's loss,
Better it be by fruits of labor than by double cross.
As we move forward in an ever-connected framework,
Let us not besmirch but get ahead through teamwork.

Terrorism

Those who would do their neighbor an injury
Usually cause misery, at least on the periphery.
Normally, terrorism is accompanied by violence,
Usually for political gain through frightening.

We are all cognizant of London and 9/11,
And we all know about the ambushes in Paris.
These are world crimes against civilians
And against the body's nature and rules of law.

But not all of us are aware of terrorism on a daily basis
Where the body is afraid of free thought,
Where state-sanctioned terrorism braces
And puts hearts and minds into a period of stasis.

Political freedom embraces all that is mainstream,
And unfair activities are natural for the regime.
Damage done to others can cause the body much trauma
But enlivens and perpetuates the rules' dogma.

In the autocracy, there is much social impiety,
And better to be on the winning side
or even in a secret society
Than to bring oneself the kind of notoriety
That causes one to shudder at the thought
of decorum and propriety.

To those nations who espouse civil liberties,
They will attract migration for the possibilities
But cannot usually interfere with a regime's facilities,
And history has shown that liberty lasts
and bitter policies die fast.

Emotional and psychological abuse
from neighbor to neighbor
Makes the body tired and the nation
weak from so much labor.
When one cannot trust another for majority favor,
The state's goodwill and balance become graver and graver.

Even in the hierarchy of nations, there is law in nature.
Logic is not always humane by concept,
As necessity regulates what must be done,
But honesty of content is basic for character.

As the world becomes more connected and symmetric,
Terrorism will wane as we can reflect on affect.
Audience is a right of law and nature.
And it is the duty of humanity to find an amicable manner.

Environmentalism

It is in all our natures to seek safety and security.
Protecting the natural world from harm shows maturity.
Protection of ambassadors can be just
as important as saving bears.
We all want where we reside to be green and take pride.

A balance between humans and natural systems is the crux,
And as the world evolves, it is in constant flux.
We want our transportation and our utilities,
But we need our activity to provide responsible availabilities.

The environment can be fragile and innocent,
And climate change in transit is significant.
We have worked hard to curtail a growing pollution,
And ultimately, we are obliged to account
for our acts and solutions.

We need our fuels, and we need our power,
But convenience alone cannot be a
barometer of kilowatts per hour.
Answers must serve purpose and function for the body.
All jurisdictions and nations have a
stake to be more than gaudy

Violators of human rights must include our outdoor nature
And use the sequels of history to do constantly greater.
We have all been entrusted to do what we can.
The honor system must maintain a safe haven.

Preservation and conservation must have a manner
That provides a refuge and sanctuary of common banner.
The environment is an affair for all mankind,
And the commerce of human nature should be so resigned.

Our common humanity is a balance and a network,
So our ecology must work above and below the earth
And, to the extent that we can all be connected,
Must fuse a philosophy and plan that is protective.

No one wants to be judged guilty of killing the landscape,
As now we know that injury to that
which is common to all
Can change the course of our convex and shape,
And nature's revenge can throw us a curve ball.

So it is a motive of humankind to show affection
And take the future movement in the right direction.
There must be acceptable sacrifices
To make public expense worth the price.

Selected UN Nation-States
(Internet Censorship)

Internet censorship is control of what
can be accessed online.
Some say free speech is being maligned,
But much of the body and nation takes an interest
In sites that do not add to morals and fitness.

Internet censorship varies from nation to nation.
Each has its own reasons or relation to sensation;
For some, it's political, religious, or familiar.
Others filter content to stop a possible killer.

While most agree that Internet access is a basic right,
Freedom of expression can come with some blight.
More people in more places now use the Internet.
Communications and commonality have
never been faster or such a threat.

Some censorship is needed to prevent evildoing,
As freedom of expression can sometimes be fooling.
But for the most part, we all have a right to know,
And it is in our nature's will and thoughts to allow the flow.

We should, by nature, have the right to disagree,
As it humanizes us and protects our basic guarantees.
The Internet plays a vital role in shaping society.
Responsibility and propriety should lessen our anxiety.

Afghanistan has been a member state since 1946.
It is an Islamic republic with opium traffics.
Only one in ten Afghans gets to go online,
As misinformation about Islam may
influence the youth to realign.

Albania has been in the UN group since '55.
The state controls the Internet, which is just fine.
There are a few restrictions for morality and a little filtering.
Expressionism is strong, and connectivity is in full swing.

Algeria is part of Arab North Africa
And is the tenth-largest country in the world.
Islam is predominant, but many have
converted due to drama.
The Internet is technically unrestricted,
But government control over order can get you convicted.

Argentina is a large republic in South America
Where Internet regulation is focused on child porn.
The body and nation are well connected,
And with free expression, there are few forlorn.

Armenia is a former Soviet Republic state,
Predominantly Christian but not a heavyweight.
Access to the Internet is mostly unconstrained,
Although their human-rights record can be blamed.

Australia is an ocean-locked country from down under.
Its Internet policies allow for one to discover.
Hard-core content is reason for blacklisting,
But there are still plenty of listings still existing.

Austria respects freedom of speech and the press.
As in Mozart's day, the nation shows progress.
Peaceful expression is publicly encouraged,
And judicial oversight prevents the inciteful from a flourish.

The Bahamas are an island nation east of the Florida Keys.
Things are at ease in Nassau, all with a warm breeze.
Access to the Internet is mostly unrestricted,
But they try to keep out the bad and wicked.

Belgium is a kingdom located in Western Europe.
Its capital is Brussels, which brings reassurance
Internet is a top-level domain with a country code.
Content can be blocked with warrants as the mode.

Belize is on the eastern coast of Central America.
The capital is Belmopan, and English speaking is typical.
The Internet has little oversight except for public safety
And helps communication maintain its integrity.

Brazil is the largest nation-state in South America.
The capital is Brasilia, and Portuguese is spoken as heritage.
The Internet has little or no governmental restrictions
But for offending the dignity or decorum of officials.

Burundi is landlocked in the Great Lakes region of East Africa.
Bujumbura is the capital, and it is populated to the maxima.
Its Internet is used by just 1 percent of the population,
As it is one of the poorest countries in the United Nations.

Chile is a South American, long, narrow strip of land.
Santiago is the capital, but it has fjords and islands.
The Internet is monitored for child porn,
But otherwise, freedom of speech is still adorned.

China is the world's most populous country.
Beijing is the capital, and a permanent UN
member for more than half a century.
China's Internet is substantially censored,
And violations will get you more than just censured.

Colombia is in northwest South America on the coast.
Drug trafficking and corruption are
prevalent in the capital of Bogota.
The Internet is heavily filtered, sorted, and streamed,
But peace and human rights have made progress a theme.

Costa Rica is a middle country in Central America.
San Jose is the capital of this neutral part of Latina.
Its Internet has no government restrictions per se,
But things like libel can get you a jail sentence anyway.

Cuba is a series of islands in the Caribbean Sea.
The capital, Havana, is only about two
hundred miles from Miami.
The country is communist ruled and just
now reopening as tensions cool.
With fewer computers per person, Cuba
is the most censored in the world.

Denmark is the southernmost Scandinavian country.
Copenhagen is a capital where people feel free.
Denmark has one of the biggest
Internet services in the world.
It is also well filtered and watches for
forces of the underworld.

Ecuador is in South America, right at the equator.
Quito is the capital city and is the highest in elevation.
Although restricted, YouTube is free and open.
Government stability is maintained, while unspoken.

Egypt covers the northeast corner of Africa.
It is Mediterranean and transcontinental with Asia.
Cairo is the capital with an Internet only partially free.
Threats, arrests, and harassment in the
Islamic state are easy to see.

El Salvador is the smallest but most populated
country in Central America.
San Salvador is the capital and considered a global city.
The Internet depends on self-reporting all the gritty,
And fear of retaliation by gangs is not arbitrary.

Ethiopia is a nation-state on the East Horn of Africa.
The largest city, Addis Ababa, is also the capital.
Its Internet is behind the times, especially socially.
Censorship is extensive and probative, with little diplomacy.

Fiji is an island nation in the South Pacific Ocean.
Suva, the political and admin capital, is always open.
Although no official restrictions on public access,
Citizens' e-mails can easily be suppressed.

Finland is the northernmost Scandinavian state.
Helsinki is the capital and considered first rate.
There is no evidence of Internet
filtering by the government,
But it is said that secret blocking by the
police helps keep its covenants.

France is one of the five permanent members
of the UN Security Council.
Paris, the City of Lights, is a place considered to be special.
France promotes a free but civilized Internet;
Encryption used against them has caused much regret.

Germany is the most populous UN
country and is an economic force.
Berlin is rich in history, and capital of the Norse.
The Internet is mostly free but for child porno,
And their filtering tries to make it an automatic no-no.

Greece, the Hellenic Republic, is in southeastern Europe.
Athens, its capital, was the beginning of brains and braun.
Its Internet is not governmentally restricted and is secure,
But police surveillance is legal, and
its long arms seem a cure.

Guatemala is a Spanish republic in Central America.
Guatemala City (Guate) has been home
to great Mayan originals.
Internet disputes are heard in the "court of honor,"
And journalists are encouraged to have a correct demeanor.

Haiti is a chain of islands in the Caribbean.
Port au Prince is the capital and very deprived.
Less than 5 percent have access to the Internet.
This nation is poor, some say corrupt, and well into debt.

Honduras is a republic in Central
America on the Pacific side.
Tegucigalpa is the capital and boasts much pride.
Reprisals from organized crime are always a fear.
That brings Internet censorship to quash all smears.

Hungary is in Europe, in the East.
Budapest is large and nice, at the very least.
The Internet is rated free, but there is conflict over security.
But Hungary tries to limit any interference with privacy.

Iceland is a Nordic island in the North Atlantic and Arctic.
Reykjavik is the capital, and it has a tundra climate.
Censorship of the Internet is prohibited.
Safeguards against child porno, terrorism,
and libel need to be protected.

India is in South Asia with more than one billion people.
New Delhi is the capital and is a pluralistic committal.
Its Internet is rated partly free.
Selective censorship prevents users from being too carefree.

Iran is a state in Western Asia, bordered by Armenia.
Tehran is the capital and Islam the mania.
They are considered an enemy of the Internet,
And it's easy to be imprisoned, so you had better fret.

Iraq is bordered by Turkey to the North and Iran to the East.
Baghdad is the capital with Arabs and Kurds as living beasts.
One can get seven years for insulting the government,
So watch your p's and q's when surfing for content.

Ireland is an island in the North Atlantic Ocean.
Dublin is the capital, and Catholicism the devotion.
Internet censorship is a controversial issue on the isle,
But they try to keep it free while securely they compile.

Israel is a Hebrew state in Western Asia and the Middle East.
Jerusalem is the capital, with Jewish and Arab populous pieced.
Its Internet, like all, prevents child porn
And is otherwise free but for terrorist encrypted suborned.

Italy is parliamentary and in the heart of the Med.
Rome is the capital, where the Vatican is also spread.
Its Internet is rated free with filtering for child porn,
And antiterrorism is utmost to be forewarned.

Japan is an island country in the Asian Pacific.
Tokyo is the capital with a populous that is quite prolific.
Without any government restrictions on the Internet,
Freedom stops with copyright infringement and child threats.

Jordan is an Arab kingdom in Western Asia.
Amman is the capital and receptive to migrant aphasia.
The Internet is only partly free due to national security,
As they live in proximity to countries of differing verity.

Kenya is in East Africa along the Equator.
Nairobi is the capital and home to its legislators.
The Internet is filtered to restrict political content,
And don't dare publish anything obscene
unless you want torment.

Kuwait is on the northern edge of the Persian Gulf.
Kuwait City is the capital, and petroleum its source.
Filtered for pornography and the antireligious,
Kuwait's Internet will not put up with anything malicious.

Libya is in North Africa on the Mediterranean Sea.
Tripoli is still the capital, where life can be beastly.
The government will monitor communications and e-mail,
While social media is accessible but unreliable and frail.

Luxembourg is landlocked by Belgium, Germany, and France.
Luxembourg City is the capital and is well advanced.
Television doubles its Internet users,
But more and more are becoming everyday consumers.

Mali is French and landlocked in Western Africa.
Bamako is the capital, and the Sahara
Desert is not far from Arabica.
Anti-Islamic content is not allowed and may be blocked.
Self-censorship may be practiced to prevent being socked.

Malta is an archipelago in the Mediterranean Sea.
Valletta is the capital, and English is spoken free.
Internet censorship and surveillance are not pervasive,
As marketplace concerns respect its cyberspace.

Mexico is part of North America and stretches to Belize.
Mexico City is the capital, and a Sunday bullfight is easy.
Internet is considered partly free with no filtering,
But that doesn't mean there is no government bickering.

Morocco is one of the five North African nations.
Rabat is the capital, but Casablanca is largest in population.
Internet is partly free and has opened up a lot over the years
But recently has stated to prosecute if content tends to smear.

Namibia is located in Southwest Africa on the Atlantic.
Windhoek is the capital, many desert areas botanic.
Although there are generally no restrictions on the Internet,
Getting permission to intrude on your privacy is no sweat.

Nepal is a high country in South Asia along the Himalayas.
Kathmandu is the capital, with Hinduism as messiah.
Internet is about as free as it gets in Nepal
But cannot be taken advantage of by all.

The Netherlands, the Dutch kingdom,
is located in Western Europe.
Amsterdam is the capital, while Rotterdam
is the largest port in Europe.
Internet censorship is for child porn and copyright.
All in all, most are wide-open sites.

New Zealand is an island nation in the
South Pacific, close to Australia.
Wellington is the capital and part of Polynesia Oceania.
This nation offers voluntary Internet filtering,
And this limited dithering seems to provide less bickering.

Nicaragua is the largest country in the
Central American isthmus.
Managua is the capital and all business; the food is delicious.
No restrictions are on the Internet or most chat rooms,
But monitoring of e-mails by NGOs can be presumed.

Norway is a kingdom in the western portion
of the Scandinavian Peninsula.
Oslo is the capital of this Nordic
country and is hardly insular.
It filters child porn and blocks the Pirate Bay
And, just like other Scandinavians, watches out for the grey.

Paraguay is a landlocked country in central South America.
Asuncion is the capital, and godparents are considered prime.
The law in Paraguay provides for freedom of speech,
But journalists beware the government's wrath and reach.

Peru is a republic in western South America on the Pacific.
Lima is the capital with a spirit that is quite civic.
E-mails and chat rooms seem free of monitoring,
But lack of good service infrastructure is not very popular.

Poland is on the Baltic Sea in Central Europe.
Warsaw is the capital, very populated and good for tourists.
Petitions and protests have put an end to blocked Webs.
Now you can trend with friends and celebs.

Portugal is on the Atlantic in southwestern Europe.
Lisbon is the capital and provides a needed reassurance.
Internet access is not restricted without legal authority say.
Engagement in adverse practices will make you the prey.

Qatar is a state in Western Asia on the Arabian Peninsula.
Doha is the capital in this family-run monarchical insular.
It's selective in political and conflict Internet security.
Islam and the ruling family watch
for criticisms and impurity.

North Korea is in East Asia on the northern Korean Peninsula.
Pyongyang is the capital of the family-run totalitarian regime.
It's an Internet enemy, as one would probably expect.
Censorship and propaganda by the government go unchecked.

South Korea, referred to as Korea, is south of its counterpart.
Seoul is the capital and has become used to having families apart.
In the South, the Internet is partly free for all,
But there is substantial censorship for
purposes of political protocol.

Russia is a permanent member and is very large.
Moscow is the capital and is where the laws are discharged.
It's selective in its conflict and security Internet concerns,
And you can lose your freedom if you don't discern.

Romania is in Southeast Europe bordering on the Black Sea.
Bucharest is the capital, where the River Danube runs free.
It provides filtering to protect for child pornography,
And casino-like websites are blocked
for economic geography.

Saudi Arabia is located in Western Asia
and is second largest in Arabia.
Riyadh is the capital in this absolute
monarchy, and oil is the mania.
It's not very free when it comes to
the Internet and its politics.
Islam, drugs, gambling, and porn are kept out of the mix.

South Africa is at the southern tip off Africa, with penguins.
The capital(s) rotate according to season
since its break from England.
Internet and media freedom is respected down under,
But starting a repugnant site can be a blunder.

Switzerland is in Western Europe and
known for its neutrality.
Bern is the de facto capital, and the
banks have complicated legalities.
It has no governmental restrictions on its Internet,
But copyright infringement is still something to sweat.

Great Britain is an island nation and
permanent member of the council.
London is the capital of operations and
provides the queen's counsel.
Its Internet is rated free, although content is watched.
And the Pirate Bay infringements are definitely blocked.

Tanzania is in Central Africa on the Indian Ocean side.
Dodoma is the capital, and Kilimanjaro
soars high into the sky.
Security forces monitor the Net, phones, and private homes.
There is no freedom of speech, so better watch your tone.

The United States is a permanent UN
member of the council with veto power.
Washington, DC, is the capital, and full
of cherry blossom flowers.
The Internet is rated free and protected
by the First Amendment,
But monitoring can be vigilant, and
constraints are attendant.

Uruguay is a small country in southern
South America on the Atlantic.
Montevideo is the capital and boasts
freedom in all things economic.
Internet e-mails and chat rooms are respected in practice,
But there are also prohibitions that can impact us.

Venezuela is the northernmost country in
South America in the Caribbean.
Caracas is the capital at the Amazon
basin with a meaty cuisine.
Its Internet is partly free, but fines can be heavy.
Ten percent of a person's income seems to be the levy.

Vietnam is easternmost in Indochina
and stretches along the coast.
Hanoi is the capital of the unified land
and serves as the guidepost.
It does not have a free Internet and is quite preventive,
With social and political opposition being a disincentive.

Zimbabwe is a landlocked domain in South Africa.
Harare is the largest and capital city but with little rigor,
And has Internet considered partly free with e-mail censored.
Efforts to crack down on dissent are well centered.

Censorship, as we have just read, tries to suppress
The obscene, controversial, indecent, and excess.
Nations seem to favor what is neutral in tone,
As it helps the body and nation become fully grown.

They say it takes a village to raise a child,
So content is important and should not be reviled.
Things contrary and harmful to the public
Do not help the body, nature, or republic.

Internet communications tend to outpace
Normal advances and concepts of real-world interface.
International lines of exchange over the cyberspace
Must yet be measured by standards in place.

The virtual nature of things creates issues
Of what to restrict and what should ensue.
Time, place, and manner are still important,
And our hopes of a better life should not be shortened.

That we can speak without injuring the body
Is a rite of passage that makes the spirit more hearty.
We meet with much that affects our futures,
And good men of sense must show honor and humor.

Connected

In the forties and fifties, we had television
To keep us connected and on the same page.
At the company watercooler, it helped our decisions
And kept us together, and our ideas took center stage.

The Internet connects billions of people and ideas.
It keeps the world connected and provides us with reason.
It covers geography and industrial borders alike.
It keeps us abreast with the newest
that comes down the pike.

The Internet provides unprecedented integration.
It can bring body and nature into one nation.
While visions and cultures will always be variable,
Our outlooks and understandings will be more amiable.

We now have smartphones and smart TVs
And will soon have smart cars and smart cities.
The notion of the connected person is here,
And predictions will be optimized to increase our years.

Cross-domain interaction will help our balance,
And common platforms will increase our talents.
It will temper our roles and our changing lives
And should benefit humanity with great strides.

Therefore, for the sake of peace and bonds of faith,
This book looks to those in grades from the eighth,
For it is the next generation that must carry
The global voice and perpetuate our clarity.

Printed in the United States
By Bookmasters